CLUES
TO THE
True
You

by Julia Marsden

SCHOLASTIC INC.
New York Toronto London Auckland Sydney
Mexico City New Delhi Hong Kong

ISBN 0-439-16115-0

Published by Scholastic Inc., 555 Broadway,
New York, NY 10012.

12 11 10 9 8 7 6 5 4 3 2 0 1 2 3 4 5/0

Printed in the U.S.A.
First Scholastic printing, February 2000

Contents

Introduction

Will the True You Please Stand Up?

Have you ever wondered what makes you tick? Well, you're about to learn! Every chapter of this book will offer up a new way to find out more about yourself. Each method for tapping into your personality offers a fun and entertaining way to learn more about what motivates you and shows you ways you can put that newly gained knowledge to work for you.

But that's not all. You can also use this info to learn more about your friends and family members, too. The info you'll read is based on theories and methods that have been around for ages. But if you find that some of the descriptions don't sound exactly like you, that just goes to show what an amazingly unique individual you are and that some of the info is necessarily broad. After all, nobody can be completely categorized. That said, you'll still get a more complete picture of who you are, which can help you to get along better with the people in your life. With this mind, get set to solve some of the major mysteries of what makes you seriously exceptional!

Chapter One

The Write Stuff: The Goods on Graphology

Excuse me, may I have your autograph? It may sound a little weird, but by offering up your signature you may be revealing a whole lot about yourself to others. That's because your handwriting can reveal a lot about your emotions, your intellect, your fears, your imagination, and your strengths.

There are handwriting experts (graphologists) out there who can analyze personalities based on the way letters are shaped, how they are joined together, and the space that's created around them. This isn't some whacked-out new idea, either. Graphologists have been studying the science of handwriting for centuries. Researchers have found references to handwriting analysis dating back as far as 4500 B.C. And in A.D. 99, a Roman historian studied the emperor Augustus's handwriting in an attempt to figure the guy out!

The more modern method of analyzing handwriting got under way in 1915 due to a man named Milton Bunker. And if you're thinking this is all still sounding a little too weird, you might be interested to know that in 1981 the Library of Congress categorized handwriting analysis as a credible social science! Today psychologists tap into elements of graphology to help them figure out a person's aptitude, motivation, and personality traits. And the police, forensic experts, and even members of the FBI have used graphology to help track down criminals.

It's pretty trippy to think that the way you put down a couple of sentences on a piece of paper can reveal so much! But the fact is, graphologists claim there are over one hundred traits that can be revealed in the way a person writes. It turns out the way you write is way revealing—and graphology is the name of the game.

So, before you read any further, sign in, please. And be sure to use a pencil or a ballpoint pen, 'cause using a felt-tip pen won't reveal as much about you! Write your signature in the space below:

The scoop on your signature? Graphologists say the way you sign your name represents the way you want the world to see you or how you want to be (which can be quite different from the way you really are). Since your signature contains only some letters of the alphabet, it doesn't provide a complete picture of who you are, but it still can reveal plenty. Check out some of the secrets behind your unique signature style:

If you underline your signature with a single line: You tend to be self-confident and self-assured.

If you underline your signature with more than one line: You seek attention and love to be noticed.

If your signature is super-big: You like to impress people and love to socialize.

If your signature is super-showy: You are an extrovert and love to talk up a storm with your friends.

If your signature merges both your first and last names together: You have a positive outlook and count on succeeding at whatever you do.

If your signature has super-showy capital letters: You like to gain the approval of others and tend to be a little bit obsessed about your physical appearance.

If your signature has a capital letter that you extend horizontally (like the letter T, for example): You feel good about yourself and can come across as quite confident.

If your signature travels upward: You are an optimist and tend to look at the bright side of situations.

If your signature travels downward: You tend to see things from a pessimistic perspective—or it could be you're just tired.

If your signature travels upward and you've underlined it: You are practical and can make quick, smart decisions.

If you've underlined your signature in a fancy way: You are a real people person and are in your element at social events of all kinds.

Hints About Your Handwriting

Write this sentence using the lines on the next page:

The quick brown fox
jumps over the lazy dog.

In case you're wondering what the deal is with this strange sentence, it's a good one for handwriting analysis because it includes every letter of the alphabet.

Are You Under Pressure?

One of the first things graphologists try to get a read on is how much pressure you apply with your pen or pencil. And here's what the differing pressure points can mean:

If you apply heavy pressure to the page: In the same way that you left your mark on the paper, you want to make a lasting impression on the people in your life. You are a productive person and are seen by your friends as dynamic. Just as your writing seems to leave an indelible mark on the page, injustices against you tend to leave an indelible mark on your heart, and at times you find it hard to forgive and forget. You tend to keep certain things "etched in stone" in your memory and this is reflected in the way you write.

If you apply medium pressure to the page: You have lots of drive and determination, but you're also someone who's into balance. Despite all your energy, you pace yourself rather than run yourself ragged. You're not one to forget about the importance of refueling by taking some time for relaxation. You're a total believer in the mind and the body needing time to recharge. But look out, world, when you're up and running, you can be a record breaker!

If you apply barely-there pressure to the page: You are adaptable and easygoing, but your energy level can evaporate pretty fast. And if you feel super-stressed, you tend to withdraw or pull away. If your writing is super-light, it could be you're soft-spoken and may even be a little anxious about your day-to-day routine. Try to tap into those worrisome feelings and use some of that nervous energy to spur yourself on when it comes to things that really interest you.

Are You Size Wise?

Graphologists study the size of writing for clues about a person's need for recognition. So keep reading to find out if you're a get-noticed kind of girl or someone who's more comfortable being behind the scenes.

Do You Have Large Writing?

If your writing takes up lots of space, you are someone who probably looks at life with lots of enthusiasm and confidence. People see you as courageous and bold. You don't mind being the center of attention and are self-confident. You probably have some pretty big plans for the future and are ambitious enough to pull off just about anything you try.

Do You Have Medium-Sized Writing?

If your writing is average in size, it is by no means a sign that you're an average or ordinary person! Far from it. You're someone who is down-to-earth, practical, and adaptable. Rather than obsessing over stuff you can't control, you tend to have a balanced approach to life. You don't feel you have to take center stage but that doesn't mean you stay back in the wings, either. You love to be involved with people and events, but you don't feel the need to always be the leader of the pack.

Do You Have Small Writing?

If your writing is small, you are probably a pretty introspective person. You take your time getting to know new people, but once you've got a sense of who they are, you're the first to be a friend. You are organized and have a keen eye for details. And don't think that small writing means you're trying to hide from the world. You are super-independent and have lots of confidence in yourself, but you value your privacy.

Are You All Lined Up?

Check out what graphologists discover when they read between the lines.

Jumbled lines: If your style of writing gets kind of caught up in itself with lots of overlapping and parts of letters latching onto letters on the next line, your life may be so busy that you don't have much time to separate out all your interests and activities. Your life runs 24/7 and if you could make it happen, you'd shoot for 24/8! You much prefer an action-packed schedule to one that strikes you as having too many empty spaces.

Average line spacing: You have a balanced and organized routine to your life. You are good at planning ahead and making time for everything you sign on to do. You even build in blocks of time to play catch-up so that you're never so stressed out that you're just trying to keep your head above water. Your smart moves enable you to remain calm and cool when your classmates are caught up in complete craziness come test time. You like to remain flexible and are super-adaptable.

Distant line spacing: If you put a lot of space between your words and the lines of what you write, you're someone who really needs her space. Rather than getting super-chummy with someone right away, you're more inclined to take your time getting to know a person. You're the queen of contemplation and like to give yourself lots of time to think things through and contemplate how you'll handle a situation. While others may feel comfortable winging it, you're the kind of girl who prefers coming up with an organized approach.

Utilizing space available: If the way you write seems to take up every little bit of available space, you may have a need to be heard. You can find it difficult to adhere to directions and rules that you feel limit or constrain you. You find it hard to let go of things, especially when you have a disagreement with someone you care about. While you're always immersed in all kinds of things, you may be prone to filling up more time than is necessary with busywork instead of focusing on the down-and-dirty details of matters of serious substance.

Are You Spacing Out?

If you have narrow word spacing in which every word you write seems to almost bump into the words on either side of it: You are a social person and like to feel connected to others in all that you do. You've even been known to introduce yourself into situations where perhaps you're not meant to be included! You can become so caught up in being part of a group that you may be prone to hanging out with people who really aren't worth your time.

If you have average word spacing in which each word you write seems to have a balanced bit of space on either side of it: You've got a good sense of balance when it comes to time spent with your buds. You are into talking with them about all kinds of things, but you also treasure the time you spend on your own. Super-self-assured, you don't have a problem giving people their space. You're perceptive about when your opinion is really wanted and when it's best to steer clear rather than interfere.

If you have wide word spacing where you put quite a bit of space between the words you write: It could be that you prefer to distance yourself from people. You've been known to retreat and pull away when someone comes on too strong. You're super-sensitive to a person's need for privacy. However, it could work to your advantage to get to know people a bit better.

Are You Well-Connected?

If MOST of the letters in each of your words are NOT connected: You tend to be impulsive, creative, and freethinking. At times, you can be kind of impractical.

If SOME of the letters in each of your words ARE connected: You have a cool, balanced way of applying your imagination and your intuition when it comes to solving tricky situations.

If ALL of the letters in each of your words ARE connected: You are someone who tends to be organized and dependable.

Are You Well-Read?

If you have writing that's easy to read: You love to communicate with others and want people to always have a clear sense of what you're trying to say.

If you have writing that's hard to read or almost indecipherable: You may be someone who is either super-busy or super-secretive!

Are You Interested in Knowing More?

Graphologists have the goods on the way you write every single letter of the alphabet. And you'd better believe they pay attention to whether or not you cross your t's and dot your i's! If you'd like to learn more about graphology, check out books at your local library or use the Internet. One cool graphology book that's geared to young readers is called *Handwriting Analysis: Can You Read Your Character?* and it's by Jacqui Tew. You may even want to contact a graphologist for a full-on handwriting analysis. It can lead to learning even more about your personality and why you do the things you do.

Chapter Two

What's Your Number? Nine Essentials

If you've heard of Hollywood, you've heard of typecasting. Well, let's skip the Tinseltown talk. There's a completely different kind of typecasting that goes on in the world of psychology. Here's how it works: Some experts believe there are nine basic personalities that comprise a personality profile model called the enneagram. In Greek, ***ennea*** means "nine" and ***gram*** means "model." Want a visual? The enneagram is a nine-pointed starlike symbol. To get a sense of where you might fall into place on the enneagram model, read the following passages and choose the one that sounds most like you. Oh, and here's a hint: If you narrow it down to a few of the passages but can't quite make up your mind about which one's for you, think about which category your friends or family members would select as the one that describes you best. Ready? Read on!

1. I'm someone who sets super-high standards for myself. I can be critical of myself and others because I like to see things done the right way. Some people might call me a perfectionist, but I figure if I'm going to do something, I want to do it right. I can get caught up in assignments for school and make a big deal out of the details. It helps when my teachers give me some feedback on things I'm working on, because it makes me feel like I'm on the right track.

2. I'm someone who is supportive and likes to get along with everybody. I try to be friendly to everyone. I hate when people argue and disagree. I've been told I care too much about what other people think. I like to help people figure out ways to accomplish their goals, but sometimes I end up putting my dreams on hold while I'm helping out everyone else. I love being around people and get kind of edgy if I spend too much time on my own.

3. I'm someone who is very into getting things done. Being successful at what I do is very important to me. I hate failing at things and work extra hard at anything I take on. I thrive on competition and expect people to pull their own weight. I

have to make a point to make time to relax and just hang out with friends, because I tend to be super-dedicated and driven by my goals.

4. I'm someone who likes to support my friends, especially when they are going through tough times. I've been told I can be super-sensitive and that I'm an incurable romantic. I probably spend too much time thinking about the future and about things that might be missing from my life rather than focusing on all the good stuff that's going on right now.

5. I'm someone who likes to watch what others are into. Some people might see me as shy or detached, but I need time on my own to figure out my feelings. I appreciate it when things happen according to schedule. A sense of structure and order in my life makes me feel more secure. I've been told I put different parts of my life into separate compartments, but it's just a way I have of keeping things consistent and under control.

6. I'm someone who likes to ask a lot of questions and sometimes I find it hard to play by the rules. I set high goals for myself and have been told that I can be kind of suspicious of others. People might see me as kind of a skeptic and maybe even a little cynical, but I like to challenge the ways things are done, especially when it seems that people aren't being treated fairly.

7. I'm someone who likes to look at life as one big adventure. I love to plan for the future and brainstorm all kinds of ideas. I've been told I'm very enthusiastic and people sometimes joke about my energy level. I'm always totally up for trying new things. If I get into trouble with someone, I'm pretty good at talking my way back into his or her good graces.

8. I'm someone who likes to lead the way. People have said I have a take-charge attitude. Sometimes I find it hard to work with others if it appears that they are slowing things down for me. I have kind of an all-or-nothing approach to life.

9. I'm someone who likes it when everyone gets along. I try to keep the peace when friends of mine are arguing. I've been told that I often ride the fence rather than take a side, but that's because I always prefer to give peace a chance, even if it means appearing wishy-washy about taking a stand. I try to provide support to people and clear the air of conflict.

Now that you've chosen the number that sounds most like you, read up on your personality profile, which follows.

One: *The Perfectionist*

As a One, it's important to you to do things right. You totally hate being criticized or punished for being wrong. You tend to be a perfectionist, detail-oriented, and super-critical of yourself and others. You're always working at trying to improve yourself and it's incredibly important to you that people are honest. You can spend a lot of time comparing yourself to your friends and can come across as kind of critical. You usually feel there is a "right" way to do things and it bugs you big-time if things veer from the way you think they should be. You work hard, and your classmates like having you as part of the group when the teacher asks students to work together.

Two: *The Giver*

As a Two, you are seen as a gentle, caring person. Your pals feel fortunate to have you as a friend. You are incredibly tuned in to their feelings and are always there to offer support. It's through your friendships that you feel important. You're big on bonding and sharing your feelings. The way you feel about yourself is totally tied in to how closely connected you're feeling to the people in your life. This is a cool quality, but you have a tendency to ignore your own wants and needs. Try to be as good a friend to yourself as you are to others. And the weird flip side of your true-blue-friend persona is that you can be manipulative in the way you deal with people. If people don't respond quite the way you want, you've been known to pout or even become kind of accusatory.

Three: *The Achiever*

As a Three, you are efficient and competent. You like to be seen as a productive person and wish you could just click your heels together and make the world run more efficiently. You love finishing up big projects and accomplishing goals you set for yourself. You feel great when you get praise from people and, though you kind of hate to admit it, you've been known to buy into the idea that image is everything. In terms of your appearance, you love to look good and feel strongly that how you present yourself to the world really does matter.

Four: *The Romantic*

As a Four, you tend to focus on all the things you don't have going on rather than on all the cool stuff that's already in your life. Rather than reveling in all that's awesome about the here-and-now, you tend to spend a lot of time engaged in wishful thinking about the future. You consider yourself to be a romantic and artistic person. You find it easy to express your feelings to those you care about.

Five: *The Observer*

As a Five, you are attracted to knowledge and learning. You want to understand the world and what makes it tick. Rather than risk feeling tapped out or drained by an intense social scene, you'll isolate yourself or get totally lost in thought so you don't have to surround yourself with people all the time. You're self-sufficient and don't need a lot of fancy stuff in your life. Instead of gifts and gadgets, people would be wise to just give you lots of space.

Six: *The Analyzer*

As a Six, you have an active imagination, and you like to look at situations from all angles rather than just taking things at face value. You can be doubtful and often ask your friends to back up what they say. You "read" people very well and have a finely tuned radar when it comes to spotting people who seem full of themselves or are prone to bending the truth. Though you are seen as someone who is very dependable, you also tend to procrastinate.

Seven: *The Adventurer*

As a Seven, you are an eternal optimist and firmly believe the sky's the limit. You hate feeling fenced in and are always itching to bust out of boring old routines. If something new and different is going on in town, you can be found at the front of the line. You've got tons of interests (and friends) and find it hard to focus on just one thing you enjoy. You've been known to completely overbook your calendar because you hate to say no to any social activities.

Eight: *The Boss*

As an Eight, you are big on being in control and can come across as kind of domineering. People who act weak or helpless can grate on your nerves. You believe people should always present themselves as strong and capable. You are super-resistant to admitting to any vulnerabilities of your own. You are a big believer in justice being served. If things don't appear fair, you can become quite direct and confrontational in your attempt to set things straight.

Nine: *The Mediator*

As a Nine, you pride yourself on being able to see situations from all sides. You like peace and harmony to prevail. People see you as someone who is caring and kind and who tries to create a comfortable environment for others. You can come across as ambivalent when asked to take sides, and when you get angry you have a tendency to keep it inside rather than risk rocking the boat.

Here's a quick look at the major pros and cons of each number and how your number affects other areas of your life.

One: *The Perfectionist*

What rates: You are conscientious and principled. You strive to live up to high ideals.

What grates: You can come across as judgmental and critical of others.

Friend factors: You are a loyal and dedicated friend and others value your sense of humor.

Career clues: Since you're efficient and organized, analytical jobs in the fields of science and law enforcement could be good picks. Health care professions are worth looking into if you consider yourself to be a people person.

Say this to yourself: "I'm still okay if I make mistakes."

Type tip: Stress less by allowing for plenty of laughter in your life. Your tendency to take things so seriously can mean you don't make much time for fun. Also, cut back on cutting remarks that you sometimes make when you're feeling under pressure. The key to true success includes allowing yourself to lighten up more.

Two: *The Giver*

What rates: You are warm and sensitive toward others.

What grates: You can be overly accommodating and indirect.

Friend factors: People love your playful and warm personality.

Career clues: Since you're a natural people person, a career in care giving professions suits you to a T. Consider becoming a counselor, teacher, or health care professional.

Say this to yourself: "I need to be as supportive of myself as I am of others."

Type tip: Give yourself some of the attention that you tend to give to others. If you're feeling upset at someone and you can't quite bring yourself to say anything about it, at least write down what you're feeling so you become more aware of how often you internalize your anger.

Three: *The Achiever*

What rates: You are energetic and goal-oriented.

What grates: You can be seen as overly competitive and self-centered.

Friend factors: You are a fun-to-be-with friend whom others look to for acceptance and positive feedback.

Career clues: Because you tend to be a hard-working, goal-oriented person, careers in business, law, computer technology, and politics may be up your alley.

Say this to yourself: "I should value my feelings as much as my accomplishments."

Type tip: Take time to reflect on your successes. Also, get involved in an activity you value that doesn't involve scoring points or getting good grades. Consider volunteer work, where the focus is on giving to others rather than receiving an evaluation for expert performance.

Four: *The Romantic*

What rates: You are sensitive and perceptive.

What grates: You can come across as moody and self-absorbed.

Friend factors: Friends see you as someone who is super-empathetic and supportive.

Career clues: You have the ability to influence and inspire. Consider jobs in the arts or working with the written word. Becoming a psychologist or counselor could also be your calling.

Say this to yourself: "I need to appreciate the present."

Type tip: Focus on the here and now rather than on the future by discovering ways to make everyday activities a little bit more exciting. You thrive on expressing your creativity, so tap into ways you can channel your ideas into something artistic. Be direct with the people in your life when it comes to expressing what you want and don't want.

Five: *The Observer*

What rates: You are curious and love to learn.

What grates: You can be seen as stubborn and negative.

Friend factors: People appreciate the fact that you are open-minded and trustworthy.

Career clues: You have a mind that can operate from a very technical or scientific perspective. Consider jobs that utilize your strong analytical and problem-solving abilities.

Say this to yourself: "I should spend more time interacting with others."

Type tip: Work on becoming less self-conscious and more uninhibited. If you are hesitant to join up with a group, remind yourself that you have the right to set clear limits and defend yourself when you feel you are being judged unfairly.

Six: *The Analyzer*

What rates: You are responsible and trustworthy.

What grates: You can be unpredictable and defensive.

Friend factors: You are seen as someone who is honest and reliable.

Career clues: Consider a career in the justice system, the corporate world, or academia.

Say this to yourself: "I need to trust my decisions and believe in myself."

Type tip: Take notice of the positive things people say about you and work hard to believe them. And don't forget to pat yourself on the back occasionally—because you don't always have to wait to hear praise from other people.

Seven: *The Adventurer*

What rates: You are an optimist and full of energy.

What grates: You can come across as restless and impulsive.

Friend factors: Friends love the way that you encourage them to be more adventurous and try new things.

Career clues: You should avoid any jobs that are super-repetitive and strive to work in a field that will allow you to travel and vary your routine.

Say this to yourself: "I need to value what I have right now."

Type tip: Focus on perfecting your ability to follow through on things you sign on for. By putting all your great ideas into action, you'll see others flock to your side to support you. Just be sure to ask others what they want from situations, too. You tend to see things only from your own perspective and need to remember that sometimes other people are involved and their opinions matter, too.

Eight: *The Boss*

What rates: You are self-confident and self-reliant.

What grates: You can be domineering and controlling.

Friend factors: Friends appreciate your straightforward approach to life.

Career clues: Look to jobs that will allow you to be a leader. Becoming an entrepreneur, business executive, or lawyer could be for you.

Say this to yourself: "I should practice compromising more often."

Type tip: Look before you leap, and think before you take action. Your impulsive nature can intimidate others. It's okay to show the world that you also have a vulnerable side.

Nine: *The Mediator*

What rates: You are supportive and upbeat.

What grates: You can come across as spacey and forgetful.

Friend factors: Friends see you as someone who is nonjudgmental and helpful.

Career clues: Consider jobs that allow you to be a diplomat or mediator.

Say this to yourself: "I will speak up for what I want."

Type tip: Instead of going along with the crowd, ask others to join you in some of your interests. And instead of answering with a middle-of-the-road "I don't know," take a stand and make a decision that conveys a definitive sense of direction.

Chapter Three

Face It: What Your Face Says About You

Grab a mirror and take a good look at your face. Then prepare to find out the messages your mug sends out to others. We're not talking about something as elementary as the difference between a smile and a frown. We can all figure that out. What you're about to read up on is something called *personology,* or *face reading.* Personologists (face readers) study how facial traits relate to personality traits and to how people think, feel, and act. To get a read on your face, choose the best description of your features in each category that follows. The clues reveal themselves beginning at the top of your head all the way down to the tip of your chinny chin chin.

The Hair Facts

If you have thick hair: You prefer the freedom of the outdoors rather than the confinement of being forced to remain inside.

If you have fine hair: You can be super-sensitive and can be easily hurt by what others say.

If you have unruly hair: You have a carefree persona and love to explore new places. Your sense of style comes more from action rather than appearance.

If you have super-short hair: You are a no-nonsense girl who is super-comfortable with herself and feels confident.

If you wear your hair long and stick-straight: You like to appear as if you're not caught up in trends but actually you are very aware of what's considered current and you tend to adopt the up-to-the-minute looks for your locks.

If your hair is super-styled: You are detail-oriented and love to have a clear understanding of things.

At the Forefront

If you have a curved forehead that appears to be kind of rounded when you pose for a side profile: You're way into creature comforts and are sometimes seen as kind of a homebody.

If your forehead area has an oval shape to it: You're seen as a forever friend because people see you as someone they can trust.

If your forehead area has a square shape to it: You like to cover all bases and take on new things.

If your forehead area has a rectangular shape to it: You are someone who is seen as being very reliable.

If your forehead area has a wide, smooth shape to it: You are a very creative and artistic individual.

Face Facts

To get a good read on the overall shape of your face, stand in front of a mirror and determine what the outline of your face looks like to you. If you're struggling to decide, whip out some lipstick and trace your face shape onto the mirror. Then step back and decide what shape now appears on the mirror's surface. (Big-time advice: If you use this method, be sure to clean the mirror using some glass cleaner when you're done.)

If you have a very round or circular face: You are super-ambitious and self-confident.

If you have a diamond-shaped face, in which your cheekbone area seems wider than your forehead and chin region: You are warm and friendly and people see you as someone who brings them lots of luck.

If you have a rectangular face (your face is long with fairly uniform forehead and chin areas): You are incredibly perceptive and are able to show lots of self-restraint.

If you have a square face (your forehead and chin area seem to match in terms of their width): You are trustworthy and honest and like to have a sense of balance in your life. You don't hesitate when making major decisions.

If you have a triangular face (your forehead is wide in comparison to your cheeks and chin): You are very determined and may be known as a bit of a flirt.

If you have a wide jaw and a narrow forehead: You are driven and have set some serious goals for yourself.

If you have a wide forehead and a squared chin: You are very creative and like to surround yourself with peaceful people.

If you have prominent cheekbones: You have a strong character and persevere long after most people give up. You are able to rally even after experiencing a setback.

Eyebrow Insights

If you have high-set eyebrows: You tend to be very choosy and selective and can come across as someone with discriminating tastes.

If you have low-set eyebrows: You are into people who show their emotions and have touchy-feely tendencies when you're trying to help them solve their problems.

If your eyebrows are naturally arched in a way that resembles a boomerang: You are very quick to make up your mind.

If your eyebrows naturally slope upward from the bridge of your nose: You show good judgment when faced with major decisions.

If you have naturally full eyebrows: You are physically strong and have a determined nature.

All Ears

If you have low-set ears (closer to your mouth than higher up near your eyes): You can come across as someone who is incredibly idealistic. People can find it difficult to live up to your expectations.

If you have fleshy earlobes that are not attached to the side of your head: You have a tendency to hang on to things that have a lot of sentimental value to you. The drawback is that some people would describe you as a major packrat!

If you have small or barely-there earlobes that are attached to the side of your head: You tend to be organized and prefer to follow set routines.

If you have ears that stick out a bit: You are super-tolerant, and people tend to turn to you when they need some encouragement.

If you have large ears: You are sensitive to people who feel they aren't part of the group, and you are encouraging to people who need to be motivated.

Eyewitness News

If you have large eyes: You are a romantic and are full of energy. You also have an active imagination.

If you have small eyes: You are curious by nature and love to try new things. On the downside, you can be impatient.

If you have average-sized eyes: You are thoughtful and a good listener.

If you have deep-set eyes: You are reflective and observant and tend to take things very seriously.

If you have close-set eyes: You can have a short fuse and can be easily irritated.

If you have wide-set eyes: You are very perceptive and tend to be very tuned in to what other people need.

If the whites of your eyes are visible below your irises: You are someone who is very sensitive and tend to get your feelings hurt easily.

Getting Nosy

If you have a long nose: You are ambitious, generous, and proud. You also have an incredibly sensitive side.

If you have a small nose: You are very imaginative and creative. You can be quite an idealist and want to make the world a better place.

If you have a large nose: You are seen as someone who is very reliable and you have an active, enthusiastic attitude toward life.

If you have a super-straight nose: You are very loyal and have the ability to make well-thought-out choices.

If you have an upturned nose: You are happy and optimistic but are sometimes seen as being a bit gullible.

If you have a nose that points downward: You like to lead the way and be in charge.

Give 'Em Some Lip!

If you have thin lips (think Courtney Cox): You're good at controlling your emotions and keeping your true feelings under wraps.

If you have wide lips (think Julia Roberts): You have a happy disposition but can suffer from spells of jealousy.

If you have small lips (think James Van Der Beek): You are more inclined to operate using your head rather than your heart.

If you have down-turned lips (think Will Smith): You can be a bit of a skeptic and are secretly quite proud of all the things you've accomplished.

If you have a full lower lip with a regular upper lip (think Ricky Martin): You are seen as someone who is very giving and generous.

If you have protruding lips (think Ryan Phillippe): You can be impulsive and have been known to change your mind at the last minute.

If you have a thin lower lip with a regular upper lip (think Gwyneth Paltrow): You can be superfrugal, but some may see you as kind of cheap.

If you have a thin upper lip with a regular lower lip (think Sarah Michelle Gellar): You are very careful about what you say and how it may be interpreted.

If you have full lips (think Michelle Williams): You love to talk up a storm and are seen as someone who's super-social.

Chin City

If you have a pointed chin (picture Jennifer Aniston): You sometimes keep your feelings to yourself and have a tough time working under pressure.

If you have a receding chin (picture Alicia Silverstone): You like to try new things but have been known to lose your nerve.

If you have a protruding chin (picture Jennifer Love Hewitt): You are a go-getter and aren't hesitant to engage in a full-on debate when it comes to topics you feel strongly about.

If you have a square chin (picture Neve Campbell): You are determined and can be set in your ways.

If you have a rounded chin (picture Drew Barrymore): You tend to be grounded and down-to-earth.

If you have a long chin (picture Alyssa Milano): You are big on the people in your life being majorly loyal.

If you have a cleft in your chin (picture Juliette Lewis): You love being the center of attention.

Give Yourself a Hand!

Now that you've figured out a thing or two based on your face, you can clue in to more about your personality by taking a look at the palm of your hand. Here's how: Flip up your hand so you're looking at your palm. Your hand description will put you in one of four categories: Earth, Air, Fire or Water.

If you have a square palm and short fingers: You have Earth hands. You're someone who is super-loyal and supportive. You are sincere and very dedicated to your friends.

If you have a square palm and long fingers with rounded fingertips: You have Air hands. You can come across as kind of aloof, but once people get to know you, you're someone whom everyone loves to be around. In fact, some friends might even get annoyed with all the people who tend to flock to you.

If you have a long palm with short, wide fingers: You have Fire hands. You can be kind of insecure. Your moods can swing from happy to sad in a couple of nanoseconds, but your friends love you because you are always there for them and come across as someone who really cares.

If you have a long palm with long fingers and kind of pointed fingertips: You have Water hands. You're way romantic and super-sensitive. You can be kind of clueless about certain things, but you're a great listener and people often turn to you for advice and support.

While just about everybody on the planet would agree that your overall appearance is due in large part to genetics, when you take a personologist's perspective, you can see how certain character traits and behaviors can be influenced by your overall combination of facial attributes. You might find that some of your personality traits can be played up, and there may be others you'll want to play down. No matter what you find, getting a read on your facial features is another great way to find out more about the true you.

Chapter Four

Hue News: The Color Connection

Psychologists use color and color preferences to learn all kinds of things about people. And marketing experts spend millions of dollars each year trying to figure out which hues will help them sell their products. The truth is, colors go to work on our psyches and cause us to see and respond to things in certain ways. Don't believe it? Well, check this out. Pink has always been perceived as a color that soothes. So, armed with that knowledge, researchers decided to paint jail cells in Seattle pink in an attempt to tone down inmates' aggression. Not only were the prisoners housed in the pink jail cells much mellower, they stayed mellower for at least half an hour after being moved from the pink cells! So, the next time you know you may be meeting up with someone who might come on strong with her opinions, put on some pink to help her chill.

Still not a believer in the power of color? Well, here's more proof. Studies have shown time and again that males respond to red in a big way. It seems seeing red registers in a guy's brain, releasing a hormone that causes his heart to beat faster and his body temperature to rise. The people who study how colors can affect people claim that the human response to red is an inborn trait. And how about a bit of background on blue? Navy blue has always been identified as a color that people associate with responsibility and trust. It's no wonder bankers have been known to suit up in navy blue suits and police officers all over the country wear dark blue uniforms.

Clue In to What Your Palette Picks Say About You

The key to answering these questions is to respond quickly. Your initial reactions are what really count. Here are the colors for you to choose from:

- Red
- Pink
- Orange
- Yellow
- Green
- Light blue
- Dark blue

- Purple
- Brown
- Black
- White
- Gray
- Silver
- Gold

Now, here are the questions to answer. Remember to think fast. Plug in the color from the Color List that works best for you.

1. If I were a color, I'd be:
(Color clue: Your color choice doesn't necessarily need to be a color you wear a lot but instead should be one that you identify with strongly.)

2. A color that I think looks good with the color I chose for #1 is:

3. The color I like the least is:
(Color clue: Your choice should be a color that you hate to wear or feel bugged to be around.)

Now check out these color cues.

The color you chose for Question #1 is your *Identity Color.*

If you chose red: You see yourself as ambitious, full of energy, and pretty much of an extrovert. Red is viewed as a flashy and dramatic color. You love to be active and enjoy competition. You can react quickly and have been known to make snap judgments.

If you chose pink: You see yourself as someone who is loving, compassionate, and sympathetic. Pink is viewed as a very caring and feminine color. You've been known to wear your heart on your sleeve and your ability to tap into your emotions is one of your greatest strengths.

If you chose orange: You see yourself as someone who is action-oriented, organized, and prone to being kind of impatient. Orange is associated with form and structure. You like things in your life to be in order.

If you chose yellow: You see yourself as someone who is talkative, social, and people-oriented. Yellow is considered the color of communication. You are an outgoing and expressive individual.

If you chose green: You see yourself as someone who is caring, idealistic, and wants to make the world a better place. Green is believed to be the color of compassion. You have a love of nature and feel most at peace when there is a natural harmony to the things going on in your life.

If you chose light blue: You see yourself as someone who is creative and is able to tune in well to what others have to say. Light blue is thought to be one of the most creative and artistic colors. You love to use your imagination and express yourself in a variety of ways.

If you chose dark blue: You see yourself as someone who is smart, responsible, and able to fend for herself. Dark blue is associated with wisdom. You show good judgment and rely on your instincts and feelings to guide you in making important decisions.

If you chose purple: You see yourself as someone who is spiritual, has strong intuition, and is able to read others' feelings. Purple is thought to be the color of intuition and spirituality. Deep shades of purple have historically been associated with royalty. You tap into your faith to help you through struggles in your life.

If you chose brown: You see yourself as someone who is down-to-earth, honest, and practical. Brown is associated with the earth. You are someone who is supportive and stable. You enjoy nature and spending time outdoors.

If you chose black: You see yourself as someone who is independent, opinionated, and has a mind of her own. Black is seen as a powerful color but is also viewed as a color that serves as a barrier.

If you chose white: You see yourself as someone who values her independence, but you can feel lonely despite liking to spend time on your own. White is thought to be a simplistic and pure color and often signifies some kind of transition.

If you chose gray: You see yourself as someone who takes on a ton of stuff and gets very involved but yet doesn't have to be the center of attention. Gray's considered a neutral shade that is an awesome accompaniment to virtually every color under the sun. It is a great contrast color, but on its own, gray is often associated with subtle style and inner strength.

If you chose silver: You see yourself as someone who is trustworthy, romantic, and dependable. Silver is a color of significance since it's symbolic of a precious metal. Like the knight dressed in a suit of silver armor, it is a color associated with honor.

If you chose gold: You see yourself as someone who is successful and has high standards and ideals. Gold is the color that symbolizes riches and wealth.

The color you chose for Question #2 is your *Inspiration Color*. It's the shade that can improve your mood and inspire you.

If you chose red: You feel best about yourself when you stay active, compete successfully, and achieve goals that you set for yourself.

If you chose pink: You feel best about yourself when you can care for others and give and receive love.

If you chose orange: You feel best about yourself when you stay organized, tap into your energetic nature, and stay focused and productive.

If you chose yellow: You feel best about yourself when you can express yourself and socialize.

If you chose green: You feel best about yourself when you can help out others and help people to see things clearly.

If you chose light blue: You feel best about yourself when you can use your imagination and express yourself through creative outlets.

If you chose dark blue: You feel best about yourself when you can be independent and self-reliant.

If you chose purple: You feel best about yourself when you can tap into your intuition and be seen by others as someone who is sensitive and supportive.

If you chose brown: You feel best about yourself and most confident when you make a contribution to a project or activity.

If you chose black: You feel best about yourself when you meet the goals you set for yourself and are able to work independently.

If you chose white: You feel best about yourself when you can share your ideas and spend unstructured time with others.

If you chose gray: You feel best about yourself when you have plenty of time to kick back and relax.

If you chose silver: You feel best about yourself when you are able to tap into your strengths and strive toward new goals.

If you chose gold: You feel best about yourself when you can pursue your goals and take time to reap the rewards of your hard work.

The Hue That's So **Not** *You*

The color you chose for Question #3 is your *Insecurity Color.*

If you chose red: You hate to bottle up your emotions and can find it difficult to control your temper.

If you chose pink: You hate being in situations where you feel that you are dependent on people.

If you chose orange: You hate experiencing feelings of confusion or frustration.

If you chose yellow: You hate feeling that you are not living up to your own expectations.

If you chose green: You hate feeling bored.

If you chose light blue: You hate feeling that you have no time to relax.

If you chose dark blue: You hate to appear as if you've lost your cool.

If you chose purple: You hate feeling that others are trying to change your beliefs.

If you chose brown: You hate to experience feelings of worry or fear.

If you chose black: You hate to feel that you are being ignored.

If you chose white: You hate to feel on your own or cut off from others.

If you chose gray: You hate to feel that you haven't met your goals.

If you chose silver: You hate when people break their promises to you.

If you chose gold: You hate feeling that others have more opportunities than you do.

What Should I Wear?

Okay, it's Monday morning. You're running late. You're staring into your closet, on the verge of having a major meltdown because you're not sure what to wear to school. Hey, it happens to everybody. But here's the good news. When you're really wigging out about your wardrobe, let the colors in your closet come to the rescue. Depending on the mood you're in or the mood you want to create for yourself, let hues have their say. Here's the color-coded clothesline:

Red says: "I want to be noticed."

Wear red when you want to feel stronger physically, be seen as powerful, and stand out in a crowd.

Pink says: "I like to care for others."

Wear pink when you want to de-stress (or de-stress others), feel feminine, and tune in to your heart.

Orange says: "I'm organized and like to get things done."

Wear orange when you want to feel organized, motivate yourself, and boost your stamina.

Yellow says: "I love to talk and share. I have a sunny disposition."

Wear yellow when you want to communicate well, keep from feeling sad, and make a good impression.

Green **says: "I'm here to help out."**

Wear green when you want to feel independent, calm others, and project a healthful image.

Light blue **says: "I'm creative and practical."**

Wear light blue when you want to tap into your creativity, learn a lot, and zero in on your logical and analytical skills.

Dark blue **says: "I like to be in charge and make lots of decisions."**

Wear dark blue when you want to keep from feeling tired or need to rely on yourself and make wise decisions.

Purple **says: "I like to be open with my feelings and let others know that I matter."**

Wear purple when you want to feel superspiritual, tune out outside pressures, and keep from becoming overly involved in something that doesn't really interest you.

Brown **says: "I like to get things done in a practical way and I'm very hard-working."**

Wear brown when you want to feel secure, remain calm, and feel stable around people who can be unpredictable.

Black **says: "I like to call my own shots."**

Wear black when you want to protect yourself from negative outside influences, stand by your beliefs, and release fearful feelings.

White **says: "I am unique and need to have my own space."**

Wear white when you want to avoid having a negative attitude and want to communicate your personal ideas and opinions but also be open to the ideas of others.

Gray **says: "I like to listen to what others have to say but I might not join in."**

Wear gray when you want to be seen as calm, avoid negative encounters with others, and steer clear of any arguments.

***Silver* says: "I like to feel positive about myself."**

Wear silver when you want to remain hopeful, boost your self-esteem, and tap into your feelings of self-respect.

***Gold* says: "I want to accomplish all kinds of things. I'm shooting for the top."**

Wear gold when you want to experience a feeling of wealth, motivate yourself, and feel secure.

Room with a Hue

If you're considering a color makeover for your room, keep these palette pointers in mind.

- **DO** decorate about two-thirds of your room in various shades of your favorite color.

- **DON'T** forget to accent your room with things that incorporate all the colors of the rainbow.

- **DO** decorate about one-third of your room in your second favorite color.

- **DON'T** forget that wood, bricks, and stones bring their own colors into the equation. Select shades that will work well with any existing colors in your room.

- **DO** remember that light and pastel colors will make your room look lighter and larger.

- **DON'T** forget that white counts as a color.

- **DO** keep in mind that bright colors such as yellow, red, green, and blue can "shrink" the size of your room.

- **DON'T** ignore the fact that warm colors such as red, yellow, and orange can make a room feel warmer.

- **DO** bear in mind that cool shades such as blue, silver, and purple can create a major "chill factor."

- **DON'T** forget to express yourself through the colors you choose when you create your ideal room.

You are born with a particular hair color and eye color, but the colors you are able to choose on your own for your clothes, your hair (if you opt to switch from your natural shade), and your room are the ones that reveal the most about your own mind-set. Clue in to your color choices now and in the future, and you'll be surprised by the way colors will continue to influence you in all aspects of your life.

Chapter 5

Put It in Ink: Rorschach Test Revelations

This chapter is all about a guy who had a major interest in inkblots. Yeah, you read right. Inkblots. As in, showing splats of ink to people and then offering up all kinds of insights about 'em, depending on what they "saw" after staring at the inkblots. He called his inkblot analysis the Rorschach test, after his own name.

During the 1910s, Rorschach became very interested in psychoanalysis, which is a method of treating problems by having people talk about whatever is on their mind. In 1911 he started experimenting with the interpretation of inkblots. But he wasn't the first guy to think there was something to how people interpreted inkblots. Before Rorschach, one of the most famous people to have looked into this practice was a painter you may have heard of—a guy by the name of Leonardo da Vinci!

Though Hermann Rorschach had a hard time selling others on his ideas about inkblots, today he is recognized as having written the classic book on the topic. The funny thing is, back when he was writing about it, the public had an interest in interpreting inkblots as part of a popular parlor game called Blotto. The idea was to look at an inkblot and describe what you saw: kinda like when people look up at clouds in the sky and describe what they see. Nowadays, the Rorschach test is totally recognized as a way to plug into an individual's personality. Here's how it works: A psychologist or the person administering the test has ten large cards with inkblots printed on them. All right, it sounds strange. You're probably still thinking, How can a splat of ink reveal anything about who I am? Sure, it sounds strange, but psychologists believe what you "see" in the inkblots reveals a lot about you. The way you interpret the inkblots can reveal to the person administering the test what's on your mind or what you hope to achieve in your life. The whole premise of looking at the inkblots is for a person to provide a gut response to what she sees. So, it wouldn't really work if you got to look at the inkblots ahead of time and then took your sweet time to come up with what you believed to be "perfect" answers.

To get a sense of what taking a Rorschach test would be like, create some inkblots of your own. To make inkblots, first cover a tabletop with newspapers so things don't get too messy. Then, fold a piece of plain white paper in half. Put a small drop of ink (you can buy a small bottle in stationery stores) in the middle of the paper near the crease you've created. Fold the paper and press it together between the palms of your hands so that the ink can spread around. Open it up, and there you have it—an inkblot ready to be analyzed! Make several inkblots so you have a good sampling to work with. You can look at them from any angle that works for you. Then, for each inkblot, write down what you see on a separate piece of paper.

Inkblot Analysis

Odds are you'll have a gut response to what you see in the inkblot. You'll probably spot (no pun intended) a main image in the inkblot and then maybe some other stuff, too.

Here's some info to help you provide your own inkblot analysis:

If the main image you see is to the right of the center: It could mean you tend to focus on the future.

If the main image you see is to the left of the center: It could mean you tend to focus on the past.

If the main image you see is in the center: It could mean you tend to focus on the present.

If the main image you see focuses on the dark inkblots: Join the club. Most people see something in the blot rather than in the white background.

If the main image you see focuses on the white space: You see things differently from most and are probably a highly creative person.

If you focus your attention on the upper portion of the inkblot: Odds are you're an achiever.

If you focus on the lower portion of the inkblot: It could be there's something going on in your world that has you feeling kind of down in the dumps.

Am I Out There or What?

If you're a little worried that you're seeing things in those inkblots that seem way too out there, you can rest a little easier knowing that plenty of people end up seeing similar things in

For an instant image analysis, see if what you found is represented in this list:

An abstract idea (for example, a peace sign, a heart, an angel)
Some form of action (like a person running, an animal leaping, a rocket shooting into space, dancers facing each other)
Animals or plants (a bear, an antelope, a pine tree, a rose, a bush are examples)
Some form of danger or aggression (a shark's open mouth, a monster moving toward you)
Food (could be an ice-cream cone, an apple, a fork)
People (a clown, a man with a tall hat, a woman wearing a bonnet are examples)

→ You're probably into ideas and enjoy learning about new concepts and philosophies.

→ You tend to take action rather than just think things through.

→ You are an earth girl and love nature.

→ You may be angry with someone, or there could be something that's been bugging you a lot lately.

→ You are seen as a nurturer and like to take care of people. You also like to be taken care of by others.

→ You are very social and love to spend lots of time with others. People see you as an extrovert.

the inkblots used for the Rorschach test. Show to others the inkblots you've made and you may be surprised to find that they see some of the same things you do!

Chapter Six

Family Matters: Birth-Order Basics

Okay, you know your birthday. But another piece of the puzzle that can tell about your personality is your birth order, as in, where you fall in the family lineup. Tons of studies have been done on this topic, and you'd have to read a heap of books and journals to get the full scoop. We can't go into too much detail here, but you'll get the idea about birth-order basics. Here's the deal: Pick one of the following categories that is the closest match for where you fall in place in your family.

The Oldest (Include Yourself Here if You're the Oldest in Your Family or if You're an Only Child)

You had your parents all to yourself when you first arrived on the planet and had all kinds of attention heaped on you as a baby. Your baby album is probably bulging with every move you made during your first months of life. Odds are

Dos and Don'ts if You're the Oldest

DO *avoid taking on too much. You can wind up way over your head because you have a tendency to take on tons of activities, projects, and leadership positions. Ease up on all those events and schedule some stress-free solitude.*

DON'T *be seen as the one who always says yes. While you love to feel needed and groove on the approval of others, it's important that you know when to say enough's enough. You can't take on absolutely everything, so choose the stuff that matters to you most.*

DO *cut yourself some slack. As a firstborn, you're big on grilling yourself for not living up to your own great expectations. You love being first, the winner, the best. Pull back from that whole perfectionism thing and invest more time in simply enjoying what it is you're involved in.*

DON'T *forget to laugh! Since you love to do things well, it's hard for you to laugh at your own mistakes. Accept the fact that you can't always come across as perfect and recognize that making mistakes is one of the best ways you can learn and improve.*

DO *stand by your strong sense of organization. You may take some ribbing for all your organizational strategies, but your love of lists and penchant for planning are awesome assets that will serve you well throughout your life.*

your parents had high expectations for you and you may feel the effects of that today. It's a natural fit for you to be the leader of the pack. People tend to see you as a perfectionist and someone they can rely on. You can be counted on in a pinch. Odds are you see yourself as someone who is conscientious and well organized. You're prone to making lists to keep track of all that you've got going on, and you take your studies pretty seriously.

The Second (or Middle-Born) Child

Sandwiched smack in the middle, you're a great negotiator and peacemaker. People tend to see you as someone who is outgoing and easy to get along with. Though you probably look up to your older sibling (or siblings) in a big way, it's also important for you to do some stuff that distinguishes you. Since your older sibling probably seeks a lot of approval from the 'rents, you may be more interested in getting positive feedback from your pals. Since you have to fight for your time in the limelight, you are likely to be super-sensitive to letting everyone have a chance to be heard. You like to avoid conflict and have a ton of friends. Your independent streak can surprise people, but you have a history of feeling that at times you need

Dos and Don'ts if You're in the Middle

DO play up your serious people skills. You've got negotiating down to a fine science. Tap into this trait when you need to see things from both sides.

DON'T buy into thinking that no one cares what you have to say. As a middle child, you may feel that it's hard to be heard. Be sure to practice sharing your ideas and letting others hear your opinions.

DO tap into your "middle" management skills. Leaderships roles aren't just for firstborns. You can compromise and negotiate incredibly well and are sure to shine as a leader.

DON'T underestimate your unique ability to look at things from all sides.

DO revel in your role as someone who is socially skilled and has tons of friends.

to fend for yourself. People are often knocked for a loop by your impulsive decision-making and you are usually the first in the group to try something new or especially adventurous.

The Baby (Last Born or Youngest)

Talk about fun-loving! As the youngest in your household, you love being in the limelight and can sweet-talk your way into getting what you want. Since you're the youngest, you may get away with certain behavior that your older sibs can't. You're able to laugh at life and are often the family member who loves to ham it up. You have a carefree attitude toward life and aren't into making things more complicated than they have to be. At your worst, you can act—you've got it—babyish and moody. Others may see your impulsive nature as a sign that you're a little bit spoiled. You can twist things to your advantage and have been known to put the blame on others when things go wrong. But you have a winning way with people and are always quick to sell them on your ideas. Your charming and engaging style is refreshing to all those around you.

Dos and Don'ts if You're the Youngest

DO offer to help others. You can come across as kind of self-centered, because you tend to be doted on within your family. Offer to help out and share your time and energy with the people in your life.

DON'T forget that you've got a real gift for being charming and persuasive. Use it to your advantage, but don't take advantage of others in the process.

DO take on responsibility. Your role as the youngest can make it hard to give up being taken care of, but to be treated in a mature way you've got to act grown-up.

DON'T steal all the attention. You love being in the spotlight, but others like their fair share, too. Work on trying to incorporate others into conversations and give them time to shine.

DO remember to pick up after yourself and avoid waiting for someone who's older to come to the rescue.

Whatever Your Birth Order

- **DON'T** underestimate where you fall into place in your family. Want to know some reasons why? Some of the closest relationships you'll have throughout your entire life are gonna be with members of your family, the family you were born into. Plus, your relationships with others will likely mirror your birth order. No doubt, you'll set out and pave your own path in the years ahead, but crazy as it may sound, understanding where you fit into place in that big old family tree of yours will serve you well throughout your journey.

Chapter Seven

What's Your Type? Personality Profiles to Ponder

How's this for mother-daughter bonding? Back in the early 1900s, a woman named Katharine Briggs was studying the works of the famous Swiss psychologist Carl Jung. She had always been interested in what made people tick and, like Jung, believed that people could be classified into various personality profiles. Around 1930 she teamed up with her daughter, Isabel Briggs Myers, and together they developed a way to measure the personality differences among people. During World War II, these two women felt that people were being asked to help out during the war effort in ways that often were ill-suited to their personalities. They created the Myers-Briggs Type Indicator (MBTI); the idea behind it was that it could help to match up a person with jobs that would be good for his or her personality. Pretty cool concept. Fast forward to the here and now and the MBTI is still one of the most widely used personality profile tools around. It's been translated into a ton of different languages and is used all over the world as a way of finding out more about people and their personalities.

The Myers-Briggs Type Indicator breaks things into sixteen possible personality types. But to make it a little easier, we've broken things down into the four major categories. Here are the words and letters you'll need to know as you make your selections for each of the four categories:

Extroverted (E) or Introverted (I)
Sensing (S) or Intuitive (N)
Thinking (T) or Feeling (F)
Judging (J) or Perceiving (P)

For a quickie taste test of what a Myers-Briggs—inspired evaluation might reveal about you, read the following sentences and decide which ones sound most like you. (You can also use this info to see what kind of traits your friends have.)

Extroverts

I'm outgoing.
I get energized being around other people.
There are tons of things that interest me.

I like to stay active by talking to people and doing things.

I've been known to act impulsively.

Introverts

I prefer hanging out with people one-on-one rather than in big groups.

I refuel by spending time on my own.

I get super-involved in a few things rather than kind of involved in a ton of things.

I spend a lot of time thinking things through.

I've been known to spend way more time thinking about something than acting on it.

Did you agree with more of the Extroverted (E) statements or the Introverted (I) statements?

Sensing

I'm tuned in to all five of my senses.

I'm laid-back and like to live in the present.

I spend more time dealing with what's going on today than on planning for the future.

I tend to follow directions step-by-step and pay attention to details.

Intuitive

I've been known to rely on my sixth sense or hunches I've had.

I've been told I have an active imagination.

I tend to work in bursts rather than methodically.

I've been known to look at the big picture and tend to ignore little details.

Did you agree with more of the Sensing (S) statements or the Intuitive (N) statements?

Thinking

I like to use logic to solve problems and make decisions.

Playing by the rules and respecting laws and procedures are important to me.

I can be objective and have been told I can be critical of people.

Feeling

I tend to apply a lot of my personal values when it comes to making decisions.

It's important to me that people try to get along and are supportive of one another.

I love to receive praise and tend to be supersensitive to criticism.

Did you agree with more of the Thinking (T) statements or the Feeling (F) statements?

Judging

I've been told I'm organized and efficient.

I like to keep lists and cross things off as I complete them.

I like it when decisions are made quickly. It bugs me when a person takes a long time to make up her mind.

Perceiving

I've been told I'm pretty flexible and adaptable.

I like to keep my options open and check out new things.

It's important to me to take in a bunch of information before making a decision.

Did you agree with more of the Judging (J) statements or the Perceiving (P) statements?

What Type of Friend Are You?

Based on your answers, find out how you can tap into your type to be an even better friend.

If you're an extrovert: You can be an even better friend by remembering to really listen when your friends confide in you. Try not to instantly offer up your opinion; instead, sit back and hear what your bud has to say.

If you're an introvert: You can be an even better friend by speaking up and offering your opinion when it's requested. While you're more inclined to sit back and take in your surroundings, your silence might be perceived as a total snub. Also, when a friend shares her problems with you, be sure you don't take the problems on as your own. Your natural desire to help out can result in heaping her stresses onto yourself. You won't be as strong for your friend if you hoist her concerns onto your own shoulders.

If you're a senser: You can be an even better bud by encouraging your friends to tell it to you straight. Rather than engaging in convos that cover the map, get specific and hone in on the details. Zeroing in on what's really being said (or not said) can help you figure out your friends. If a friend is struggling with a situation that seems too big to solve, encourage her to seek out help or see if you can steer her in the right direction.

Chill-Out Chart: Feeling Frazzled?

Discover the mellow-out moves that make the most sense for your type.

EXTROVERTS: *Write in a journal and allow yourself time for reflection.*

Introverts: *Talk out your troubles with someone you feel close to.*

SENSERS: *Delve into some dream time and let your imagination ease your anxieties.*

INTUITIVES: *Do something that requires paying attention to details so that your mind can focus on something completely separate from what's bugging you.*

THINKERS: *Take the time to communicate with others in ways that don't require tons of talking.*

FEELERS: *Tell yourself there's a reward in it for you if you let your worries go.*

JUDGERS: *Stick to a to-do list or some type of visual organization tool.*

PERCEIVERS: *Give yourself plenty of time to get things done.*

If you're intuitive: You can be an even better friend by relying on your amazing perception skills. While others may want to gloss over what they see as small stuff, you have an uncanny ability to pick up on the little things that can blow up into big-time battles. Encourage friends to hammer things out so those sticky situations don't become impossible to improve upon.

If you're a thinker: You can be an even better pal by helping your friends to remain objective even when their feelings are seriously sabotaging their efforts. Suggest that your friends use their logic and reasoning skills to get to the bottom of things that are bugging them. If a friend is at her boiling point, you're the one who can help her to simmer down so she won't regret what she says.

If you're a feeler: You can be an even better pal by resisting your natural tendency to want to rescue people from their problems and turn those problems into your own. Also, friends don't always share the same values, and what seems like a perfectly smart solution to you may not work for a pal. Go ahead and put yourself in her shoes when you're trying to help her out; just remember—those shoes aren't yours.

If you're a judger: You can be an even better friend by avoiding your traditional quick-fix techniques. You may want to come to your friend with a full-on plan of action, but it may not be one she wants to use. Instead, tap into your natural ability for coming up with all kinds of options. Then let her be the one to decide how to handle things.

If you're a perceiver: You can be an even better bud by encouraging your friends to consider all their options. You are able to see all kinds of alternatives, even in situations where it seems like there's just a single solution. Voice all your ideas. Your friends will value your input.

Conclusion

The Future Is Now

After reading this book, you're probably a little more psyched about the field of psychology and excited to know more about yourself—and your friends. Hopefully these pages have helped you learn a thing or two about your unique personality, and perhaps they have even inspired you to find out more. Your curiosity and sense of fun can serve as a catalyst for further exploration.

Check out books at your local or school library or surf the Internet to find out even more about the incredible components of your personality. And remember that learning about yourself and your friends is a lifelong gig. Getting started on figuring things out now will prepare you for a seriously enlightened future.